Recorder *from the* Beginning

Blues, Rags & Boogies

John Pitts

Blues, Rags and Boogies helps to extend the range of musical forms and styles that should be available to provide enjoyment for recorder players. The selection features some well-known tunes, as well as exciting new pieces by John Pitts in authentic blues, ragtime and boogie styles.

The level of rhythmic sophistication required in some pieces may surprise the unwary, but all the items are carefully graded, both in range of notes (pitches) and level of difficulty. The incentive to perform a new piece should help develop any new skills required. The 'jazz choruses' are notated improvisations, intended to give the feeling of 'jazzing around' a tune. The book will be suitable for players who have reached the end of book 1 of *Recorder from the Beginning* upwards, in the author's widely popular teaching scheme.

The Pupil's Book includes guitar chord symbols and the Teacher's Book provides piano accompaniments for all the pieces.

The blues originated in the southern states of the USA around 1900. The main sources were the work songs and spirituals sung by the slaves, plus ragtime music – a type of early jazz that had appeared in the late 19th century (e.g. Scott Joplin's 'Maple Leaf Rag' 1899). In ragtime the melody is strongly syncopated against a steady accompaniment. Boogie-woogie was a special type of early jazz that first became popular in America in the 1920s. The pieces are usually in 12 bar sections, sometimes using 'blues' harmonies, with a repeating bass pattern and rhythmic phrases using dotted notes. A traditional 'blues' always follows the same strict chord pattern that lasts for twelve bars. The melody often uses 'blue notes' – flattened thirds and sevenths.

Chester Music Limited
part of The Music Sales Group
14–15 Berners Street, London W1T 3LJ, UK

Contents

Notes listed as included do not necessarily appear often in a piece. Some may occur only once or twice! It is best to assess each item individually.

JC Blues   John Pitts

Cherry Tree Rag   John Pitts

Woofenbacker's Boogie   John Pitts

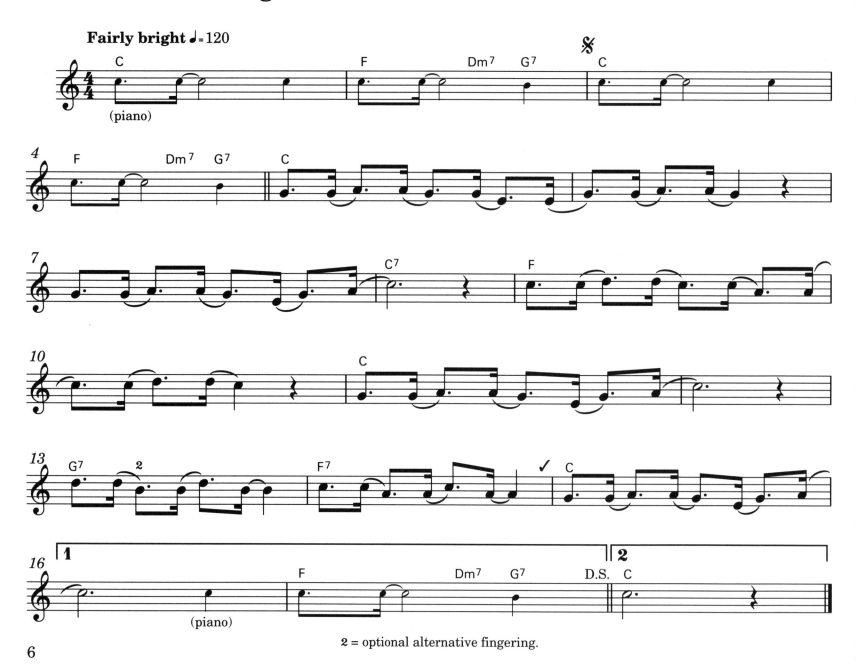

2 = optional alternative fingering.

Calverley Street Blues   John Pitts

Mo's Boogie-Woogie   John Pitts

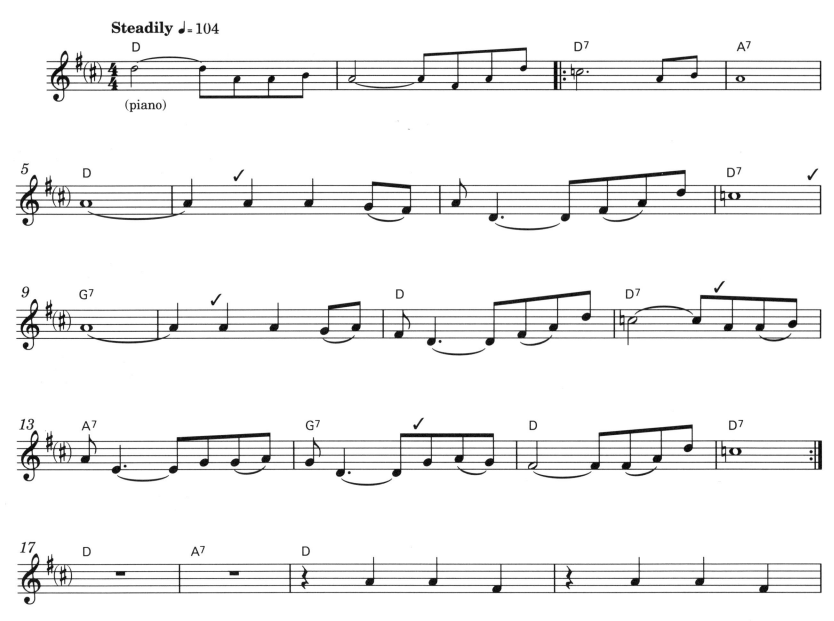

9

New River Train   Traditional

11

Rooney Rag   John Pitts

2 = optional alternative fingering.

Take This Hammer Traditional

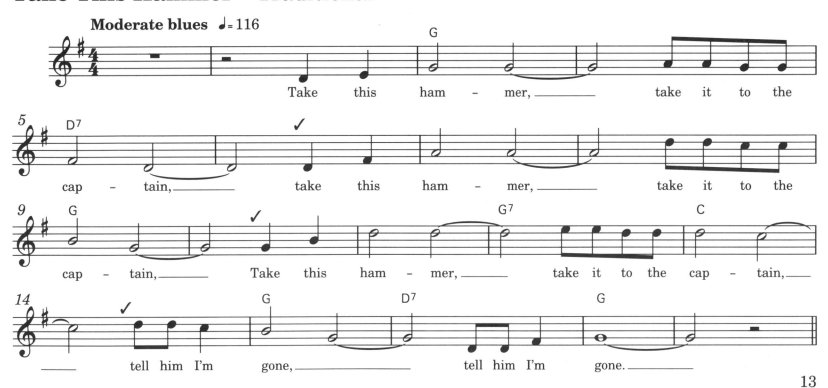

Michèle's Boogie Bounce   John Pitts

Bel's Blues   John Pitts

The Saints   Traditional

2 = optional alternative fingering.

Little Brown Jug   Traditional

Not too fast

(piano)

My wife and I lived all a-lone in a

lit-tle wood hut we called our own. She loved gin and I loved rum, I'll tell you what, we'd

lots of fun! Ha ha ha! He he he! Lit-tle brown jug don't I love thee! Ha ha ha!

He he he! Lit-tle brown jug don't I love thee!

Fine   'Jazz' chorus

(piano)

D.C. al Fine

John Henry   Traditional

Down By The Riverside   Traditional

Goin' to lay down my sword and_ shield

Down by__ the ri - ver - side, Down by__ the ri - ver - side, Down by__ the

ri - ver - side. Goin' to lay down my sword and_ shield Down by__ the ri - ver - side, Goin' to

stu - dy__ war no more.__ I ain't goin' to stu - dy_ war no

more; Ain't goin' to stu - dy_ war no more; Ain't goin' to stu - dy war no

more.____ I ain't goin' to stu - dy_ war no more; Ain't goin' to stu - dy_ war no

more. Ain't goin' to stu - dy__ war no more.____

Minty's Moody Blues   John Pitts

The Midnight Special — Traditional

Not too fast ♩=100

(piano)

Now you wake — up in the morn - ing, You hear the ding - dong ring, ____ And you go march - ing to the ta - ble, ____ You see the same old thing ____ Knife and fork on the ta - ble, But noth - ing in the pan, ____ But if you say some - thing a - bout it, ____ You're in ____ trou - ble with the man! Oh, let the Mid - night Spe - cial ____ shine her light on me, ____ Oh, let the Mid - night Spe - cial ____ shine her ev - er lov - ing light on me.

2 = optional alternative fingering.

Crombie's Boogie John Pitts

Bill Bailey Traditional

Ragtime John Pitts

24

Long-Handled Shovel Traditional

American Patrol F.W. Meacham

2 = optional alternative fingering.

Easy Winners   Scott Joplin

A Ragtime Two Step

Weeping Willow Scott Joplin

A Ragtime Two Step

Fingering Chart
English (Baroque) Fingered Recorders

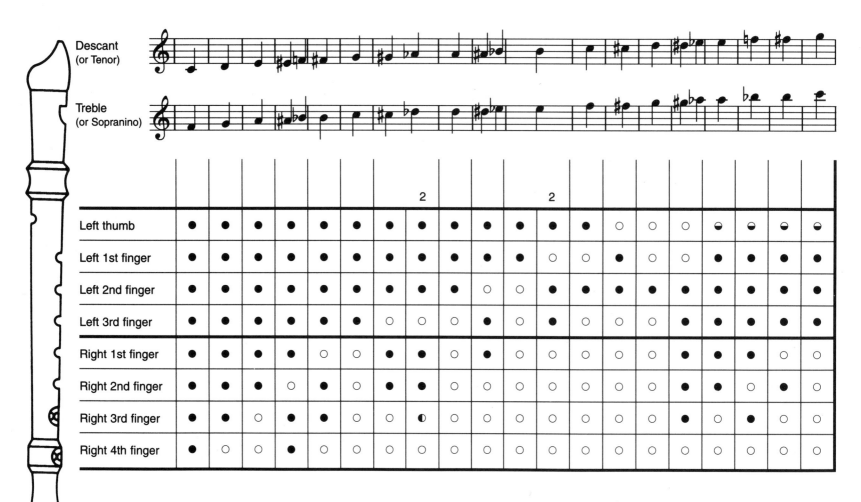

									2				2							
Left thumb	●	●	●	●	●	●	●	●	●	●	●	●	●	○	○	○	◖	◖	◖	◖
Left 1st finger	●	●	●	●	●	●	●	●	●	●	●	○	○	●	○	○	●	●	●	●
Left 2nd finger	●	●	●	●	●	●	●	●	○	○	●	●	●	●	●	●	●	●	●	●
Left 3rd finger	●	●	●	●	●	●	○	○	○	●	●	○	○	○	●	●	●	●	●	●
Right 1st finger	●	●	●	●	○	○	●	●	○	●	○	○	○	○	○	●	●	●	○	○
Right 2nd finger	●	●	●	○	●	○	●	●	○	○	○	○	○	○	○	●	●	○	●	○
Right 3rd finger	●	●	○	●	●	○	○	◑	○	○	○	○	○	○	○	●	○	●	○	○
Right 4th finger	●	○	○	●	○	○	○	○	○	○	○	○	○	○	○	○	○	○	○	○

○ Open hole

● Closed hole

◖ Partly closed hole

2 Alternative fingering

8/08(166422)